Unlimited

A 40 Day Law of Attraction Workbook to Accelerate
Manifestation

By Zehra Mahoon

I am a powerful creator
I am unlimited
I can have, be or do anything I want

~ Abraham (Abraham-Hicks)

Acknowledgements

I want to thank Abraham, and Esther & Jerry Hicks for all the work they have done and continue to do to teach the Law of Attraction and how to use it.

I have learnt much from them and as a result I have changed my life and the life of others.

Our thoughts are powerful. I always thought I was a very positive person, but I know now that wanting positive results is not the same as being positive. Knowing that difference is perhaps my biggest accomplishment in life, and my biggest gift to all those for whom I am the teacher.

I want to thank Johnhain for providing the artwork for the cover.

Much love and appreciation,
Zehra

Unlimited

A 40 Day Law of Attraction Workbook to Accelerate
Manifestation

By Zehra Mahoon

For Monisha... always remember your perfection and the power of your being.

Contents

Unlimited – Law of Attraction Coaching & Support Group

On Facebook

This is a dedicated closed group for people who are interested in support while following the 40 day workout.

It is a safe place to ask questions, share successes and bond with others who are on a similar journey. It is also a place where you can have direct access to guidance and coaching from me.

Admission to this group is free to those who purchase a copy of the book "Unlimited" between Jan 1, 2017 to Apr 30, 2017. For all others membership cost is USD50 per month.

My objective is to allow access to Law of Attraction coaching to those who for whatever reason are unable to sign up for one-on-one coaching sessions which cost USD150 per hour.

In order to gain admission to the group please email me a copy of your purchase receipt for the book, and send a request on Facebook to be added to the group.

Why I wrote this book and why you should read it

Are you like me?

Do you usually know what you need to do, but don't always do it?

Like knowing that you would benefit from going to the gym a couple of times a week or knowing that meditation helps with everything in life, but not finding the time to fit it in.

If you answered "yes" then you and I are the same.

Most people who have come across the Law of Attraction know that it would be of benefit to them to learn how to use it deliberately, but most of them don't really apply themselves to doing the work that needs to be done. Either they don't know how to use the tools or they don't make the effort to try.

Eleven years ago I made the decision that I was willing to do whatever it would take to change my life and that was when I came across the Law of Attraction. I experimented with the tools and became good at using them. I changed my life in many ways, but I did not use all the tools all the time. I used some and then I used others. Over a period of time, through experimentation I developed a formula combining some of the tools that when I used them consistently over a period of 30-40 days always yielded positive results, and my life continued to improve.

After the 40 days my use of the tools becomes intermittent as I got busy enjoying my new state of being and exploring further to give birth to more desires.

You see, I know that when I do the Law of Attraction work that is needed to be done, I always achieve a major movement forward towards the things I want – but many times I spend more time thinking about doing the work than doing the work.

Then I reach a point when I make the conscious decision that nothing is more important than doing the work, because everything I want in life is a result of doing the work. That's when I become disciplined and focused. And it doesn't take very long for things to morph to what I want. I am at that juncture in life again where I am reaching for something new, and so I have been reflecting on the tools at my disposal, and creating a mental checklist.

I started working on my 40 day plan only to discover that I needed more consistency - I was not using all the tools I had intended to. I decided a checklist to keep me on track would be a good idea, as a result this book was born.

I confess. I wrote this book for me.

This checklist of things that are part of my formula for using the Law of Attraction deliberately will serve me for many years to come. I will use it every time I want to create a shift in my life.

Then the thought occurred to me that there must be others out there who are like me – reaching for something in life, and not being disciplined in their use of the Law of Attraction – so I thought I would share my checklist with you.

This checklist will keep both you and me on track. If we can both take just 40 minutes daily for each of the next 40 days we can manifest a shift that will take us closer to all the things we want. The Universe will surprise and delight us in many ways that were not even on our list. And the impact of the work we do over the next 40 days will continue to serve up results beyond the forty days.

I know this because I have done this 40 day routine several times over the past ten years and each time it has helped me move forward in ways I could not have foreseen. I am much happier because of it, and I know for sure that I have creative control over my life because I have manifested many things that had been waiting to happen for a long time.

Why you should use this book

You should use this book if you want to create a shift in your life.

If you have been wanting things to happen, that are just not coming about.

You should use this book, if you think you understand the Law of Attraction, but are not being able to use it to create consistently good results in your life.

You should use this book if you are someone who is seeking freedom, joy and growth.

You should use this book if you want a disciplined and structured approach to using the Law of Attraction in your life.

You should use this book if you are ready to give yourself another chance at success.

You should use this book if you want to prove to yourself that you are powerful and that you have control over what happens to you in life, and that you really do know how to use the Law of Attraction to manifest the life you want to live.

How to use this book

This book is your guide for the next 40 days. You can start using it whenever you want; the important thing is to be consistent. It has to be so important to you to change your life and improve it that you do whatever it takes to get the improvement that you want.

This work book consists of two sections. Section one lays the foundations of what you need to understand about the law of attraction. Section two consists of the daily workbook that will help you to accomplish what you want.

Each day is organised into four sections:

1. How to think about your day
2. Things you need to do
3. Things you need to ask the Universe to do for you
4. Notes about your day

Completing the four sections will require a minimum commitment of 40 minutes each day.

Whether you are new to understanding and using the law of attraction or someone who is well versed, this workbook will pivot you to the next level in your growth, understanding and success.

Isn't it worth it to spend 40 minutes a day for the next 40 days to accomplish a major shift? A major movement forward?

If you answered "yes" then you are in the right place and it is time for us to begin.

Much love and appreciation,
Zehra

Section 1
Understanding the Law
of Attraction

Understanding the Law of Attraction

We don't need to understand the Law of Attraction in order to improve our lives, because we are innately equipped with a knowing of it. You can use this book without any knowledge of the Law of Attraction and get wonderful, positive results.

Here is a summary of what you need to know about the Law of Attraction. If you want to go into more detail than is offered here, you may get the book "Thrive" as a companion to this workbook.

1. The Law of Attraction is always working and it applies to everything in our life. Whether we are living a life that we want or whether our life has many things missing that we desire to have, it is all because of the law of attraction.
2. Law of Attraction is consistent and works the same way every time.
3. Whether we think about things we want or things we want to change we attract both. Law of attraction brings us what we spend time thinking about, so if we spend more time thinking about the absence of something in our life compared to the having of it, the Law of Attraction will bring us the absence of it.
4. We can take control and change things in a very short time.
5. Our beliefs form the framework of possibilities in our life – only those things can happen that we believe are possible.
6. We can only control our own outcomes, we cannot create for anyone else regardless of who they are and how much we care about them.
7. Our life is the evidence of how good a job we are doing of thinking on purpose. If things we want are missing from our life, then we need to change the way we think.

8. Wanting positive results and thinking positively are two different subjects – we all want positive results, but many of us don't know how to think positively about them.

9. When we change the way we think, our life changes – therefore we have complete control over what happens because we control our thoughts and the actions that arise from them.

10. Many times we think on autopilot, meaning we are not consciously aware of what we are thinking, and therefore we create by default rather than create deliberately.

11. Our emotions are our guidance system – they tell us if we are heading in the direction of what we want or away from it. When we feel good we are pointed in the right direction. When we feel bad, we need to take note and change what we are thinking.

12. We never have to go back into our past in order to make the future better, we can start from where ever we are and forge ahead.

13. We can have, be or do anything we want – all things are possible. Whether we see it or not, there is always a way.

14. Thinking patterns are addictive in the sense that they are habitual. In the beginning we have to exert effort to learn new ways of thinking.

15. In order to understand how the Law of Attraction works we must step away from the cause and effect relationship that applies to the physical world. Law of Attraction teaches us that our negative thoughts about one subject can have a negative impact on other subjects in our lives. In other words, positive thoughts create positive results and negative thoughts create negative results.

Goals are important

Goals are important because we must have direction. How we think about our goals is the most important thing.

When we get excited thinking about our goals, or feel confident about them then we are headed towards them. When we feel despair or doubt about being able to achieve our goals we are heading away from them.

The way we feel tells us what to do.

We never have to give up on our desires. But we do have to find a way to feel good about them. When we feel the absence of something in our lives accompanied with a strong feeling of despair, anxiety or doubt, it is important to say "even if I can't see a way at this time of how this will come about, I am willing to trust that there is a way and with time I will be led to it".

I have found that feeling goals work a lot better than doing goals or getting goals. Life is really not about the things we want. It's about how we think we will feel when we get them. So the real goal is the feeling. So intend to feel joy, success and satisfaction, rather than to get the promotion, the house, the car, or the relationship. When you intend to feel happy, then all things that make you happy must be.

Focusing on being happy as the goal allows us to keep the door of possibility open. In other words, we tell ourselves, the Universe and that which we call God, that we are willing to allow all those things into our lives that will give us joy and satisfaction. You see, sometimes we think something will make us happy, but really when we get it we find out that it wasn't really what we wanted because it did not bring with it the feeling that we wanted to feel. So let the ultimate goal be the feeling of joy; the feeling of success and achievement; the feeling of satisfaction.

There is something screwy about doing this work in order to get material results.

When you do this 40 day workout because you want to create movement on some specific thing, you shoot yourself in the foot, because when you notice how far you are from your goal, the Law of Attraction expands the distance between where you are and what you want. It is best to do the work to improve your life overall and in the process all things that you want will enter easily into your life.

Here is what we intend to achieve at the end of our 40 day Law of Attraction Workout.

"It is my positive intention to create a shift in my life that will open new doors and allow my wellbeing to flow. I want to achieve improvement in all aspects of my life. I want more abundance, more health, more love, move confidence, more joy, more satisfaction, more confidence. I want to feel in control of my life. I want to feel good. As I start this journey I am willing to learn and to be open to all good things that are waiting for me."

The role of gratitude and appreciation

Gratitude and appreciation are important tools. When we appreciate we feel better, and when we feel better good things happen. Law of attraction says that the way we feel attracts what happens next. When we feel good more good things come. Gratitude and appreciation are all about feeling blessed, feeling good and therefore attracting more good.

Living in the now means always looking for something that feels good in the now moment. Life is a string of moments. A string of good moments is a happy and fulfilled life. Being conscious means being aware of how we are thinking.

When we start understanding that appreciation is the key to getting everything we want, we start looking for things to appreciate and as we appreciate our life changes – it doesn't take long... 40 days is plenty.

As we embark on this journey, we need to remember that appreciation is not limited to the time we spend doing our exercises; it is something we need to practice as much as we can during the day so that we become habitual appreciators. But starting our day with appreciation is important because it sets us off on the right foot, and good start improves the odds of good finish. That is why we will start each of the next 40 days by finding at least five things to appreciate.

Sometimes we are at a place in our life where it is hard to find anything to appreciate about where we are. If you feel this way, then it will be of value to you to look outside of your life to find things to appreciate. Look towards nature. It is always possible to find something about nature to appreciate. The sky, the trees, the grass, the birds, the flowers, the sparkly snow, the warm cheerful sunlight, the water flowing in the brooks and streams – these are all the things that we can appreciate freely. The more often we think thoughts of appreciation, the closer we get to all the things we want.

Whether you feel appreciation for the blue sky or the money in your wallet, the feeling of appreciation is the same, and it is the fuel that propels us towards the things we want. Any excuse for feeling the feeling of appreciation is good enough.

The role of meditation

Meditation is an important part of this 40 day workout.

Meditation is a process that creates clear space in our hearts and minds and allows clarity of thought which leads to better decisions which lead to better results. Meditation creates a short cut that allows improvement to take place at a faster pace, and that is why it is important to incorporate it in our 40 day workout.

Even if you have never before sat down to meditate you can learn quickly and easily. The key is to remember that there is no such thing as a bad meditation or meditation done wrong.

Simply explained, meditation is the process of holding on to the space between two thoughts. It is not the process of eliminating thought. We cannot stop thinking – it would be the equivalent of telling our heart to stop pumping blood. Our brains will do what they were meant to do.

When we focus our attention on a simple unemotional thought such as listening to the sound of our breath or repeating a string of words, it is easier to slip into and hold on to the space between two repetitions of the same thought – and that really all there is to the process of meditation.

Sit in a quiet place when you have ten to fifteen minutes to be by yourself. Intend to meditate and allow your guidance to flow through, leading you towards all the things that you want, without becoming specific about them. Focus on your breathing or repeat simple words such as "breathe in love, breathe out appreciation" and when a different thought comes into your mind, set it aside and return to your breath or your mantra. This will keep you anchored in your meditation. Accept that thoughts will come, and trust that you have the ability to return to your anchor and re-enter the space between your thoughts. You can also use a guided meditation, there are several available for free on YouTube. I enjoy silent meditation the most, however, from time to time I will also use the guided meditation tracks by Abraham-Hicks, Jose de Silva or Dr. Wayne Dyer.

If you would like to learn more about meditation you can pick up the book "Peace Within". It simplifies the process of meditation, and you will find it easy to read as well as to put into practice.

The role of affirmations

In our 40 day workout we start each day with an affirmation. The purpose is to keep the suggested affirmation top of mind for the day and to keep remembering to return to it several times during the day.

An affirmation is simply a positive thought that keeps us pointed in the direction of better feeling emotions. I know from personal experience that affirmations don't always work. That happens in cases where the affirmation contains words that magnify where we are rather than where we want to go.

For example affirming "I am a millionaire" when your bank balance is zero, has the possibility of making you feel good because as you speak the words you feel the feeling of abundance or it can make you feel bad by magnifying the absence of the million dollars in your life.

There are two things to remember when using affirmations: 1) feel the feeling of possibility, of hope as you say the words, 2) use an affirmation that is general enough that it feels believable to you.

The affirmations used in this book are deliberately general. Accept them and believe them to be true statements. When you do so you plant new empowering beliefs that will help keep the door of possibilities open.

The role of visualization

Visualization has been used for a very long time as a tool to help people achieve their goals – but it doesn't work consistently for everyone. If it did, we'd all be using it to get everything we want. That's because the process of visualization does not apply the same way to every situation.

How we feel about the goal we want to achieve has a lot to do with what to put in the visualization. I will not get into the details of how visualization works but just remember one thing: if your goal feels unachievable or really difficult to achieve then your visualization should not be detailed. Under all circumstances the best visualizations are ones that focus on how you want to feel, without incorporating any sort of detail about what has to happen to get you there.

You see when you become specific about how you want things to work out, you rule out the fact that the Universe might have a better plan for you – a better way of making things work out.

The best visualization is to close your eyes and just allow yourself to feel the joy of knowing that everything in your life is good and that you are in the perfect place. You can visualize telling a friend "I feel so happy and blessed, my life is really, really good", and feel how that would feel, without putting conditions or limitations on it – without saying "this and this and this has to happen and then I will feel good".

Creating a new belief system

Our beliefs form the basis from which we think our thoughts. Therefore each thought we think has roots linked to multiple beliefs.

We don't need to probe into our beliefs in order to change them – we could, but it is not necessary. This is because when we adopt new beliefs our old beliefs become inactive and fade away. It's our use of the beliefs that keeps them alive. So in order to adopt new empowering beliefs all we have to do is to choose them, and then use them as a guide to the thoughts we think.

For example, if I have decided that my new belief about life is "anything is possible" then I must always refer back to this belief in my logic. So when I think the thought "wouldn't it be nice if I could go on a cruise holiday", my old habit might be to say "ah… that's probably never going to happen", but if I refer to my chosen new belief then I would say "anything is possible, so there is a possibility that I may be able to take a cruise holiday". Or "it's flue season, I could get sick" versus "it's flue season, but anything is possible so I could stay healthy all season".

The more air time I give my chosen new belief, the stronger it gets and the stronger it gets, the more natural it becomes for me to think thoughts that are congruent with it, and the happier I feel, and the happier I feel the better my life becomes. At the end of the day what we all want is to achieve freedom. Freedom to have, be or do anything we want – we want to be unlimited, and any thought that interferes with that possibility is a negative thought.

So you see, we all want positive results, but we don't always think about things in a positive empowering manner. Knowing that difference and starting to consciously and deliberately think positive thoughts is the key to the power of the Law of Attraction. A simple way to tell if you are being positive is to check how you feel. When you feel good, you are being positive and when you feel bad, you are being negative.

In the creation process our thoughts act like magnets. When we think good feeling positive thoughts, we attract good things, people and events and when we think bad feeling negative thoughts we attract things, people and events that we do not want.

If you want to delve further into this aspect of the Law of Attraction, I recommend you read the book "Thrive". It contains a set of 40 illustrations that explain how the law of attraction works.

The most important belief of all, the one belief that can change our life is:

"All things are possible"

Just because you can't see how doesn't mean that they're not – there is always a way. Keep the door of possibility open – always.

Pre-paving or setting your intention

Pre-paving is another term that implies setting our intention. When we set our intention we make a decision about what we want. The clearer our intention the stronger our power of focus the higher the probability that things will play out the way we want them to.

Pre-paving is not about telling the Universe or God what you want, because God already knows. Pre-paving is about telling yourself where you want to hold your focus and what sort of thoughts you want to think. Make sense?

So when we say something like "I want to have a good day" we are basically telling ourselves to look for good things in our day.

When we pre-pave "I want my interaction with this person to go well" we're basically telling ourselves to focus on things going well.

"Where attention goes, energy flows."

When we focus on things going well with a feeling of expectation, we direct our energy to a positive outcome, and that is what creates a positive outcome.

Deadlines and accepting outcomes

Deadlines that are difficult to achieve give birth to negative thoughts. Therefore, deadlines are dangerous because they can keep things from happening.

Think about it. If you have a deadline for something, and you can't see yourself achieving it, does that feel good or bad. If it feels bad then you know that you are thinking in opposition to the empowering belief "all things are possible".

The reason I bring this up is because this is a 40 day workout. I want you to understand that this does not apply a 40 day deadline to manifesting anything. If you approach this work with the attitude of achieving something within a deadline, then you might as well not start at all. Attention to the deadline is in opposition to the belief "all things are possible" because every time you look at the deadline and observe how far or close it is you are focusing on the shortage of time. The shortage of time or anything else is a negative thought. Focusing on something negative cannot yield positive results.

Approach this 40 day plan with the attitude of trust. Trust that anything is possible. Remind yourself that it is possible for no evidence or manifestation to show up for 39 days and 23.5 hours, and then everything that you have been wanting can show up in the last half hour. Remind yourself that if something that you want is not coming to you then it is for no other reason than that you are thinking in opposition to it, so keep repeating to yourself "anything is possible".
I have observed that when I keep score of the 40 days and nothing happens – it is because I have been looking for evidence and then as soon as I give up looking everything falls into place. That could be on day 45 or 50 or 60. Looking for something too soon can keep it from coming. So don't put a 40 day deadline on anything.

Tell yourself that the 40 days of work are the key that opens the door to things coming into your experience. Sometimes, the door can open right away, much before the 40 days are done and sometimes it can take longer. Trust that the Universe and that which we call God is more powerful than we are and can bring us anything we want.

One of the things I have done in order to get past looking for evidence and deadlines is to accept the worst that can happen. When we make peace in our hearts with the worst possible outcome that our imagination and worry can serve up to us, then we become open to allowing all other possibilities. As long as we keep pushing back and saying "I don't want that" we keep generating negative energy and therefore we create the opposite outcome of what we want.

Some years ago when I was new to doing this work, I was in a place where I could lose my house to foreclosure. The best thing I could do was to accept that fact that if that happened, it would not be the end of the world. When I accepted what I thought was the worst possible outcome, I was inspired to an idea that actually helped me not only keep the house but turn things around for myself quite substantially and in a very short space of time.

Playing creation games

When I first learnt about the power of the Law of Attraction, I wanted to use it to "fix" all the things in my life that weren't going the way I wanted them to. As I embarked on the journey, I improved some subjects and made some subjects worse. It took a while before I was able to figure out why.

You see, when you don't know how to swim, jumping into the deep end is probably not such a good idea. But that is exactly what I did, and I know many others do when they learn of the Law of Attraction – we apply it to the subject in the life that we are the most stuck on, and make it worse.

It is beneficial to play light hearted creation games with yourself. Get some practice. Practice with things that are not important to you, such as manifesting a rainbow or a butterfly or a coin in the parking lot. Manifesting small things gives us the creative practice we need so that we become habitual manifestors – creating and manifesting with ease, with a knowing that all things really are possible.

Doubt is the enemy of manifestation. The more we care about the outcome the more we doubt our power to control it, and the more we doubt the more negative we go in our thoughts. The result – we get the opposite of what we want.

Playing creation games is an optional part of the 40 day workout.

The journey beings here

As with any journey before we start out we need to know where we are and where we want to go.

So take a few minutes to complete the following preliminary work.

Where I am

On a scale of one to ten, ten being best identify where you are on the following aspects of your life:

Health   _5_

Money   _5_

Relationships   _5_

Self-worth   _4_

Personality   _4_

Career   _0_

Joy   _6_

Freedom   _3_

Other subject important to me _Creative life_

Write down your intention (where you want to go)

Don't try and work on everything – just pick one subject on which you would like to see movement forward.

My positive intention with this work is to create movement forward on the subject of

_____

I am commencing this work on _____

day of _____ *, 20_____ .*

Instructions for the daily work

☐ **Pre-pave the day** – setting forth positive intentions for the day makes the day go better. It's important to stay general, and it is equally important to generate a good feeling as you say the words. I find it best to pre-pave as soon as my eyes are half open. When I started doing this work, I found it helpful to write my pre-paving on a flash card and keep it by my bedside. I would grab it first thing and read it over – fall back into sleep – come back, read it again, and read it again on my way to work. I repeat the pre-pave whenever the thought occurs to me. It is the best way to stay focused on what is positive.

Dear God, thank you for a brand new opportunity to enjoy life. I want my day to unfold with ease. I want good things to come my way. I want to remember to appreciate people, places and things. I want to be good to myself and others. I want to end this day feeling happy and satisfied. I want to remember at all times that all things are possible.

☐ **Meditate** (silent or guided, 15-20 mins)

I enjoy both silent meditation and guided meditation. On some days one works better than the other. We don't need more than 15-20 minutes of meditation each day. I like getting it in before I get to work – in fact, most days I sit in my car outside my office to do my meditation. Two kids, two cats and a dog at home with an open door policy makes the car the best possible choice for a place to meditate! The most important thing about meditation is to do it.

☐ **Five things I "Appreciate" today**

This section is important. I always knew it was important, and I always thought I could just do it in my head. What I've found is that writing my appreciation down is more powerful because it keeps me in the vibration of appreciation for longer. The important thing about appreciation is to feel the feeling of appreciation. It's the feeling that is most important – the sentence doesn't have to be long. Here is an example of what I would do.

Always remember to start your sentences with the words "I love and appreciate... "

1. I love and appreciate my children – I feel blessed to have them in my life.
2. I love and appreciate the work I do and the difference I make in people's lives.
3. I love and appreciate where I live and the opportunities that come to me.
4. I love and appreciate my ability to write and share what I know with others.
5. I love and appreciate my morning mug of coffee. I love how it smells and tastes.

☐ **Three things I want to achieve today**

These don't have to be big hairy things – small things that absolutely have to get done can be on this list. You don't have to have three things to put on the list, but put at least one item on your list.

1. I want to keep my commitments to all my clients and complete the three files on my desk today.
2. I want to make sure I do my meditation before I start work.
3. I want to attend the party at Rob's place and enjoy myself.

☐ **Three things I want the universe to achieve for me today or later.**

As before, you don't have to have three items to put on the list, but find at least one. When you hand something over to the Universe or God, don't put a deadline on it. Just hand it over and forget about it. Trust that when you are ready the Universe will deliver. Start with small things like parking places and things on your grocery list. These are things that are impacted by factors that may be outside your control.

A nice way to word these items is to begin with the words:

"Wouldn't it be nice if..."

1. Wouldn't it be nice if there is a parking spot right at the door when I get to Costco.
2. Wouldn't it be nice if some of the things on my grocery list are on sale today.
3. Wouldn't it be nice if my last appointment cancels and I can go home early.

☐ **Bless my loved ones** – if your loved ones are with you give them a hug while consciously feeling love for them. If they are not with you, visualize their happy smiling faces and send them your love.

- [ ] **Bless my work** – find something about your work that you like. I always bless my job for putting food on my table and enabling me to afford the means to do other things. I also appreciate being a teacher and helping others, as that helps me to flow energy.

- [ ] **Bless my food** – remember to be thankful for the food we eat and remember that it provides us with the sustenance we need.

- [ ] **Bless my body** – thank our body for the work it does every day without our conscious involvement. Thank our eyes, our sense of taste, our strength – so much to be appreciative of.

- [ ] **Bless my home** – so thankful to have a place to call home. Soon as I walk in through the door I feel relaxed. I love where I live.

- [ ] **Bless any other subject** in your life that you are feeling strong appreciation for – maybe it is a person, maybe it is something that has happened or about to happen, and maybe it is a beautiful blue sky or the warmth of the sun.

Depending on how much time is available we can get more detailed about our appreciation on these and other subjects. The important thing here is simply the acknowledgement that there are many things in our life that are working really well. For when we focus on things that are working, other things that we want to have work, will start working too – that is how the Law of Attraction works.

☐ **Visualization** – You can create your own visualization – keep it simple and focus on the feeling you want to feel as you experience the things you want. My visualization is simple. I see myself happy and energized with a simple thought that I am either thinking alone or sharing with someone.

"I feel so happy and blessed, my life is really, really good, I am happy where I am and reaching for more."

☐ **My thoughts at the end of this day**

Reflecting on the good things that happened during the day helps to keep positive energy moving. It doesn't have to be a long list. Even if we can take the time to remember one thing that happed during the day that makes us simile, our work is done. It is always nice to start the sentence with one of the suggested phrases given below. I'll usually say things like "it was fun talking to Linda today – she is such a wonderful person. I am so happy I know her. The easy one for me is always to reach for one of my children or one of my pets. It is always easy for me to find something about them to smile and be happy about.

I enjoyed... I am appreciative of... I am thankful for... I loved... I want more of... I want to be like...

☐ **Bed time pre-paving** – again this is something that I had on a flash card on my bedside. Of course I no longer need the flash card as I have the words memorized. Most nights I don't remember getting to the end of my pre-paving – most nights I pre-pave sitting at the edge of my bed, because as soon as I put my head down on my pillow, I am asleep.

"I am going to bed now. I want to sleep well. I want my body to relax and rejuvenate. I want to reset myself emotionally and physically. I want to wake up feeling energized and eager for my day."

☐ *If you miss a beat*

Don't worry if you can't get everything on the list checked off. The Universe will not hold you accountable. The benefit of doing all the suggested work is the acceleration of energy flowing, combined with a reduction of resistance due to the incorporation of the new belief "anything is possible". The combination of the two is what leads to accelerated manifestation. The more positive energy you flow the better life keeps getting.

Section 2
The 40 day workout

Day No. 1 ~ All things are possible

☐ Pre-pave the day

> Dear God, thank you for a brand new opportunity to enjoy life. I want my day to unfold with ease. I want good things to come my way. I want to remember to appreciate people, places and things. I want to be good to myself and others. I want to end this day feeling happy and satisfied. I want to remember at all times that all things are possible.

☐ Meditate (silent or guided, 15-20 mins)

☐ Five things I "Appreciate" today

> *I love and appreciate...*

1. _____

2. _____

3. _____

4. _____

5. _____

☐ Three things I want to achieve today

1. _____

2. _____

3. _____

34

☐ Three things I want the universe to achieve for me

1. _____

2. _____

3. _____

☐ Bless my loved ones

☐ Bless my work

☐ Bless my food

☐ Bless my body

☐ Bless my home

☐ Bless _____

☐ Visualization

"I feel so happy and blessed, my life is really, really good, I am happy where I am and reaching for more."

☐ My thoughts at the end of this day

I enjoyed... I am appreciative of... I am thankful for... I loved... I want more of... I want to be like...

_____

_____

_____

_____

_____

_____

_____

_____

_____

_____

_____

☐ Bed time pre-paving

"I am going to bed now. I want to sleep well. I want
my body to relax and rejuvenate. I want to reset
myself emotionally and physically. I want to wake up
feeling energized and eager for my day."

Day No. 2 ~ Things are always working out for me

☐ Pre-pave the day

> Dear God, thank you for a brand new opportunity to enjoy life. I want my day to unfold with ease. I want good things to come my way. I want to remember to appreciate people, places and things. I want to be good to myself and others. I want to end this day feeling happy and satisfied. I want to remember at all times that all things are possible.

☐ Meditate (silent or guided, 15-20 mins)

☐ Five things I "Appreciate" today

> *"I love and appreciate..."*

1. _____

2. _____

3. _____

4. _____

5. _____

☐ Three things I want to achieve today

1. _____

2. _____

3. _____

☐ Three things I want the universe to achieve for me

   1. _____

   2. _____

   3. _____

☐ Bless my loved ones

☐ Bless my work

☐ Bless my food

☐ Bless my body

☐ Bless my home

☐ Bless _____

☐ Visualization

> "I feel so happy and blessed, my life is really, really good, I am happy where I am and reaching for more."

☐ My thoughts at the end of this day

   I enjoyed... I am appreciative of... I am thankful for... I loved... I want more of... I want to be like...

_____

_____

_____

_____

_____

_____

_____

_____

_____

_____

_____

☐ Bed time pre-paving

"I am going to bed now. I want to sleep well. I want
my body to relax and rejuvenate. I want to reset
myself emotionally and physically. I want to wake up
feeling energized and eager for my day."

Day No. 3 ~ I am open to new ways of thinking and doing

☐ Pre-pave the day

> Dear God, thank you for a brand new opportunity to enjoy life. I want my day to unfold with ease. I want good things to come my way. I want to remember to appreciate people, places and things. I want to be good to myself and others. I want to end this day feeling happy and satisfied. I want to remember at all times that all things are possible.

☐ Meditate (silent or guided, 15-20 mins)

☐ Five things I "Appreciate" today

> *"I love and appreciate..."*

1. _____

2. _____

3. _____

4. _____

5. _____

☐ Three things I want to achieve today

1. _____

2. _____

3. _____

☐ Three things I want the universe to achieve for me

    1. _____

    2. _____

    3. _____

☐ Bless my loved ones

☐ Bless my work

☐ Bless my food

☐ Bless my body

☐ Bless my home

☐ Bless _____

☐ Visualization

    "I feel so happy and blessed, my life is really, really good, I am happy where I am and reaching for more."

☐ My thoughts at the end of this day

    I enjoyed... I am appreciative of... I am thankful for... I loved... I want more of... I want to be like...

    _____

    _____

_____

_____

_____

_____

_____

_____

_____

_____

☐   Bed time pre-paving

"I am going to bed now. I want to sleep well. I want
my body to relax and rejuvenate. I want to reset
myself emotionally and physically. I want to wake up
feeling energized and eager for my day."

Day No. 4 ~ I am willing to allow good things

☐ Pre-pave the day

> Dear God, thank you for a brand new opportunity to enjoy life. I want my day to unfold with ease. I want good things to come my way. I want to remember to appreciate people, places and things. I want to be good to myself and others. I want to end this day feeling happy and satisfied. I want to remember at all times that all things are possible.

☐ Meditate (silent or guided, 15-20 mins)

☐ Five things I "Appreciate" today

> *"I love and appreciate…"*

1. _____

2. _____

3. _____

4. _____

5. _____

☐ Three things I want to achieve today

1. _____

2. _____

3. _____

☐ Three things I want the universe to achieve for me

1. _____

2. _____

3. _____

☐ Bless my loved ones

☐ Bless my work

☐ Bless my food

☐ Bless my body

☐ Bless my home

☐ Bless _____

☐ Visualization

> "I feel so happy and blessed, my life is really, really good, I am happy where I am and reaching for more."

☐ My thoughts at the end of this day

I enjoyed... I am appreciative of... I am thankful for... I loved... I want more of... I want to be like...

_____

_____

_____

_____

_____

_____

_____

_____

_____

_____

_____

☐   Bed time pre-paving

"I am going to bed now. I want to sleep well. I want
my body to relax and rejuvenate. I want to reset
myself emotionally and physically. I want to wake up
feeling energized and eager for my day."

Day No. 5 ~ I am learning to think on purpose

☐ Pre-pave the day

> Dear God, thank you for a brand new opportunity to enjoy life. I want my day to unfold with ease. I want good things to come my way. I want to remember to appreciate people, places and things. I want to be good to myself and others. I want to end this day feeling happy and satisfied. I want to remember at all times that all things are possible.

☐ Meditate (silent or guided, 15-20 mins)

☐ Five things I "Appreciate" today

> *"I love and appreciate…"*

1. _____

2. _____

3. _____

4. _____

5. _____

☐ Three things I want to achieve today

1. _____

2. _____

3. _____

☐ Three things I want the universe to achieve for me

1. _____

2. _____

3. _____

☐ Bless my loved ones

☐ Bless my work

☐ Bless my food

☐ Bless my body

☐ Bless my home

☐ Bless _____

☐ Visualization

"I feel so happy and blessed, my life is really, really good, I am happy where I am and reaching for more."

☐ My thoughts at the end of this day

I enjoyed... I am appreciative of... I am thankful for... I loved... I want more of... I want to be like...

_____

_____

_____

_____

_____

_____

_____

_____

_____

_____

_____

☐ Bed time pre-paving

"I am going to bed now. I want to sleep well. I want my body to relax and rejuvenate. I want to reset myself emotionally and physically. I want to wake up feeling energized and eager for my day."

Day No. 6 ~ I can always find a thought that feels better

☐ Pre-pave the day

> Dear God, thank you for a brand new opportunity to enjoy life. I want my day to unfold with ease. I want good things to come my way. I want to remember to appreciate people, places and things. I want to be good to myself and others. I want to end this day feeling happy and satisfied. I want to remember at all times that all things are possible.

☐ Meditate (silent or guided, 15-20 mins)

☐ Five things I "Appreciate" today

> *"I love and appreciate..."*

1. _____

2. _____

3. _____

4. _____

5. _____

☐ Three things I want to achieve today

1. _____

2. _____

3. _____

☐ Three things I want the universe to achieve for me

1. _____

2. _____

3. _____

☐ Bless my loved ones

☐ Bless my work

☐ Bless my food

☐ Bless my body

☐ Bless my home

☐ Bless _____

☐ Visualization

"I feel so happy and blessed, my life is really, really good, I am happy where I am and reaching for more."

☐ My thoughts at the end of this day

I enjoyed... I am appreciative of... I am thankful for... I loved... I want more of... I want to be like...

_____

_____

_____

_____

_____

_____

_____

_____

_____

☐   Bed time pre-paving

"I am going to bed now. I want to sleep well. I want
my body to relax and rejuvenate. I want to reset
myself emotionally and physically. I want to wake up
feeling energized and eager for my day."

Day No. 7 ~ The future can be better than the past

☐ Pre-pave the day

> Dear God, thank you for a brand new opportunity to enjoy life. I want my day to unfold with ease. I want good things to come my way. I want to remember to appreciate people, places and things. I want to be good to myself and others. I want to end this day feeling happy and satisfied. I want to remember at all times that all things are possible.

☐ Meditate (silent or guided, 15-20 mins)

☐ Five things I "Appreciate" today

> *"I love and appreciate..."*

1. _____

2. _____

3. _____

4. _____

5. _____

☐ Three things I want to achieve today

1. _____

2. _____

3. ☐ _____

☐ Three things I want the universe to achieve for me

    1. _____

    2. _____

    3. _____

☐ Bless my loved ones

☐ Bless my work

☐ Bless my food

☐ Bless my body

☐ Bless my home

☐ Bless _____

☐ Visualization

    "I feel so happy and blessed, my life is really, really good, I am happy where I am and reaching for more."

☐ My thoughts at the end of this day

    I enjoyed... I am appreciative of... I am thankful for... I loved... I want more of... I want to be like...

    _____

    _____

_____

_____

_____

_____

_____

_____

_____

_____

_____

☐   Bed time pre-paving

"I am going to bed now. I want to sleep well. I want
my body to relax and rejuvenate. I want to reset
myself emotionally and physically. I want to wake up
feeling energized and eager for my day."

Day No. 8 ~ I want to feel my guidance

☐ Pre-pave the day

> Dear God, thank you for a brand new opportunity to enjoy life. I want my day to unfold with ease. I want good things to come my way. I want to remember to appreciate people, places and things. I want to be good to myself and others. I want to end this day feeling happy and satisfied. I want to remember at all times that all things are possible.

☐ Meditate (silent or guided, 15-20 mins)

☐ Five things I "Appreciate" today

> *"I love and appreciate…"*

1. _____

2. _____

3. _____

4. _____

5. _____

☐ Three things I want to achieve today

1. _____

2. _____

3. _____

☐ Three things I want the universe to achieve for me

1. _____

2. _____

3. _____

☐ Bless my loved ones

☐ Bless my work

☐ Bless my food

☐ Bless my body

☐ Bless my home

☐ Bless _____

☐ Visualization

"I feel so happy and blessed, my life is really, really good, I am happy where I am and reaching for more."

☐ My thoughts at the end of this day

I enjoyed... I am appreciative of... I am thankful for... I loved... I want more of... I want to be like...

_____

_____

_____

_____

_____

_____

_____

_____

_____

_____

_____

☐   Bed time pre-paving

"I am going to bed now. I want to sleep well. I want
my body to relax and rejuvenate. I want to reset
myself emotionally and physically. I want to wake up
feeling energized and eager for my day."

Day No. 9 ~ I want ease and flow on all subjects

☐ Pre-pave the day

> Dear God, thank you for a brand new opportunity to enjoy life. I want my day to unfold with ease. I want good things to come my way. I want to remember to appreciate people, places and things. I want to be good to myself and others. I want to end this day feeling happy and satisfied. I want to remember at all times that all things are possible.

☐ Meditate (silent or guided, 15-20 mins)

☐ Five things I "Appreciate" today

> *"I love and appreciate…"*

1. _____

2. _____

3. _____

4. _____

5. _____

☐ Three things I want to achieve today

1. _____

2. _____

3. _____

☐ Three things I want the universe to achieve for me

   1. _____

   2. _____

   3. _____

☐ Bless my loved ones

☐ Bless my work

☐ Bless my food

☐ Bless my body

☐ Bless my home

☐ Bless _____

☐ Visualization

   "I feel so happy and blessed, my life is really, really good, I am happy where I am and reaching for more."

☐ My thoughts at the end of this day

   I enjoyed... I am appreciative of... I am thankful for... I loved... I want more of... I want to be like...

   _____

   _____

_____

_____

_____

_____

_____

_____

_____

_____

_____

☐   Bed time pre-paving

> "I am going to bed now. I want to sleep well. I want
> my body to relax and rejuvenate. I want to reset
> myself emotionally and physically. I want to wake up
> feeling energized and eager for my day."

Day No. 10 ~ I can have, be or do anything I want

☐ Pre-pave the day

> Dear God, thank you for a brand new opportunity to enjoy life. I want my day to unfold with ease. I want good things to come my way. I want to remember to appreciate people, places and things. I want to be good to myself and others. I want to end this day feeling happy and satisfied. I want to remember at all times that all things are possible.

☐ Meditate (silent or guided, 15-20 mins)

☐ Five things I "Appreciate" today

> *"I love and appreciate..."*

1. _____

2. _____

3. _____

4. _____

5. _____

☐ Three things I want to achieve today

1. _____

2. _____

3. _____

☐ Three things I want the universe to achieve for me

1. _____

2. _____

3. _____

☐ Bless my loved ones

☐ Bless my work

☐ Bless my food

☐ Bless my body

☐ Bless my home

☐ Bless _____

☐ Visualization

"I feel so happy and blessed, my life is really, really good, I am happy where I am and reaching for more."

☐ My thoughts at the end of this day

I enjoyed... I am appreciative of... I am thankful for... I loved... I want more of... I want to be like...

_____

_____

_____

_____

_____

_____

_____

_____

_____

_____

_____

☐ Bed time pre-paving

"I am going to bed now. I want to sleep well. I want my body to relax and rejuvenate. I want to reset myself emotionally and physically. I want to wake up feeling energized and eager for my day."

Day No. 11 ~ Life is meant to feel good

☐ Pre-pave the day

> Dear God, thank you for a brand new opportunity to enjoy life. I want my day to unfold with ease. I want good things to come my way. I want to remember to appreciate people, places and things. I want to be good to myself and others. I want to end this day feeling happy and satisfied. I want to remember at all times that all things are possible.

☐ Meditate (silent or guided, 15-20 mins)

☐ Five things I "Appreciate" today

> *"I love and appreciate..."*

1. _____

2. _____

3. _____

4. _____

5. _____

☐ Three things I want to achieve today

1. _____

2. _____

3. _____

☐ Three things I want the universe to achieve for me

1. _____

2. _____

3. _____

☐ Bless my loved ones

☐ Bless my work

☐ Bless my food

☐ Bless my body

☐ Bless my home

☐ Bless _____

☐ Visualization

"I feel so happy and blessed, my life is really, really good, I am happy where I am and reaching for more."

☐ My thoughts at the end of this day

I enjoyed... I am appreciative of... I am thankful for... I loved... I want more of... I want to be like...

_____

_____

_____

_____

_____

_____

_____

_____

_____

_____

_____

☐   Bed time pre-paving

"I am going to bed now. I want to sleep well. I want
my body to relax and rejuvenate. I want to reset
myself emotionally and physically. I want to wake up
feeling energized and eager for my day."

Day No. 12 ~ I want to feel good

☐ Pre-pave the day

>   Dear God, thank you for a brand new opportunity to
>   enjoy life. I want my day to unfold with ease. I want
>   good things to come my way. I want to remember to
>   appreciate people, places and things. I want to be
>   good to myself and others. I want to end this day
>   feeling happy and satisfied. I want to remember at all
>   times that all things are possible.

☐ Meditate (silent or guided, 15-20 mins)

☐ Five things I "Appreciate" today

>   *"I love and appreciate..."*

1. _____

2. _____

3. _____

4. _____

5. _____

☐ Three things I want to achieve today

1. _____

2. _____

3. _____

☐ Three things I want the universe to achieve for me

1. _____

2. _____

3. _____

☐ Bless my loved ones

☐ Bless my work

☐ Bless my food

☐ Bless my body

☐ Bless my home

☐ Bless _____

☐ Visualization

"I feel so happy and blessed, my life is really, really good, I am happy where I am and reaching for more."

☐ My thoughts at the end of this day

I enjoyed... I am appreciative of... I am thankful for... I loved... I want more of... I want to be like...

_____

_____

_____

_____

_____

_____

_____

_____

_____

_____

_____

☐ Bed time pre-paving

"I am going to bed now. I want to sleep well. I want my body to relax and rejuvenate. I want to reset myself emotionally and physically. I want to wake up feeling energized and eager for my day."

Day No. 13 ~ I want to feel my guidance

☐ Pre-pave the day

> Dear God, thank you for a brand new opportunity to enjoy life. I want my day to unfold with ease. I want good things to come my way. I want to remember to appreciate people, places and things. I want to be good to myself and others. I want to end this day feeling happy and satisfied. I want to remember at all times that all things are possible.

☐ Meditate (silent or guided, 15-20 mins)

☐ Five things I "Appreciate" today

> *"I love and appreciate…"*

1. _____

2. _____

3. _____

4. _____

5. _____

☐ Three things I want to achieve today

1. _____

2. _____

3. _____

☐ Three things I want the universe to achieve for me

1. _____

2. _____

3. _____

☐ Bless my loved ones

☐ Bless my work

☐ Bless my food

☐ Bless my body

☐ Bless my home

☐ Bless _____

☐ Visualization

"I feel so happy and blessed, my life is really, really good, I am happy where I am and reaching for more."

☐ My thoughts at the end of this day

I enjoyed... I am appreciative of... I am thankful for... I loved... I want more of... I want to be like...

_____

_____

_____

_____

_____

_____

_____

_____

_____

_____

_____

☐ Bed time pre-paving

"I am going to bed now. I want to sleep well. I want my body to relax and rejuvenate. I want to reset myself emotionally and physically. I want to wake up feeling energized and eager for my day."

Day No. 14 ~ It is as easy to create a castle as a button

☐ Pre-pave the day

> Dear God, thank you for a brand new opportunity to enjoy life. I want my day to unfold with ease. I want good things to come my way. I want to remember to appreciate people, places and things. I want to be good to myself and others. I want to end this day feeling happy and satisfied. I want to remember at all times that all things are possible.

☐ Meditate (silent or guided, 15-20 mins)

☐ Five things I "Appreciate" today

> *"I love and appreciate..."*

1. _____

2. _____

3. _____

4. _____

5. _____

☐ Three things I want to achieve today

1. _____

2. _____

3. _____

☐ Three things I want the universe to achieve for me

1. _____

2. _____

3. _____

☐ Bless my loved ones

☐ Bless my work

☐ Bless my food

☐ Bless my body

☐ Bless my home

☐ Bless _____

☐ Visualization

"I feel so happy and blessed, my life is really, really good, I am happy where I am and reaching for more."

☐ My thoughts at the end of this day

I enjoyed... I am appreciative of... I am thankful for... I loved... I want more of... I want to be like...

_____

_____

_____

_____

_____

_____

_____

_____

_____

_____

☐ Bed time pre-paving

"I am going to bed now. I want to sleep well. I want
my body to relax and rejuvenate. I want to reset
myself emotionally and physically. I want to wake up
feeling energized and eager for my day."

Day No.15 ~ I want to feel my power

☐ Pre-pave the day

> Dear God, thank you for a brand new opportunity to enjoy life. I want my day to unfold with ease. I want good things to come my way. I want to remember to appreciate people, places and things. I want to be good to myself and others. I want to end this day feeling happy and satisfied. I want to remember at all times that all things are possible.

☐ Meditate (silent or guided, 15-20 mins)

☐ Five things I "Appreciate" today

> *"I love and appreciate..."*

1. _____

2. _____

3. _____

4. _____

5. _____

☐ Three things I want to achieve today

1. _____

2. _____

3. _____

☐ Three things I want the universe to achieve for me

1. _____

2. _____

3. _____

☐ Bless my loved ones

☐ Bless my work

☐ Bless my food

☐ Bless my body

☐ Bless my home

☐ Bless _____

☐ Visualization

> "I feel so happy and blessed, my life is really, really good, I am happy where I am and reaching for more."

☐ My thoughts at the end of this day

> I enjoyed... I am appreciative of... I am thankful for... I loved... I want more of... I want to be like...

_____

_____

_____

_____

_____

_____

_____

_____

_____

_____

_____

☐   Bed time pre-paving

"I am going to bed now. I want to sleep well. I want
my body to relax and rejuvenate. I want to reset
myself emotionally and physically. I want to wake up
feeling energized and eager for my day."

Day No. 16 ~ The future can be better than the past

☐ Pre-pave the day

> Dear God, thank you for a brand new opportunity to enjoy life. I want my day to unfold with ease. I want good things to come my way. I want to remember to appreciate people, places and things. I want to be good to myself and others. I want to end this day feeling happy and satisfied. I want to remember at all times that all things are possible.

☐ Meditate (silent or guided, 15-20 mins)

☐ Five things I "Appreciate" today

> *"I love and appreciate..."*

1. _____

2. _____

3. _____

4. _____

5. _____

☐ Three things I want to achieve today

1. _____

2. _____

3. _____

☐ Three things I want the universe to achieve for me

1. _____

2. _____

3. _____

☐ Bless my loved ones

☐ Bless my work

☐ Bless my food

☐ Bless my body

☐ Bless my home

☐ Bless _____

☐ Visualization

"I feel so happy and blessed, my life is really, really good, I am happy where I am and reaching for more."

☐ My thoughts at the end of this day

I enjoyed... I am appreciative of... I am thankful for... I loved... I want more of... I want to be like...

_____

_____

_____

_____

_____

_____

_____

_____

_____

_____

☐   Bed time pre-paving

"I am going to bed now. I want to sleep well. I want
my body to relax and rejuvenate. I want to reset
myself emotionally and physically. I want to wake up
feeling energized and eager for my day."

Day No. 17 ~ I am unlimited

☐ Pre-pave the day

> Dear God, thank you for a brand new opportunity to enjoy life. I want my day to unfold with ease. I want good things to come my way. I want to remember to appreciate people, places and things. I want to be good to myself and others. I want to end this day feeling happy and satisfied. I want to remember at all times that all things are possible.

☐ Meditate (silent or guided, 15-20 mins)

☐ Five things I "Appreciate" today

1. _____

2. _____

3. _____

4. _____

5. _____

☐ Three things I want to achieve today

1. _____

2. _____

3. _____

☐ Three things I want the universe to achieve for me

1. _____

2. _____

3. _____

☐ Bless my loved ones

☐ Bless my work

☐ Bless my food

☐ Bless my body

☐ Bless my home

☐ Bless _____

☐ Visualization

"I feel so happy and blessed, my life is really, really good, I am happy where I am and reaching for more."

☐ My thoughts at the end of this day

I enjoyed... I am appreciative of... I am thankful for... I loved... I want more of... I want to be like...

_____

_____

_____

_____

_____

_____

_____

_____

_____

_____

_____

☐   Bed time pre-paving

"I am going to bed now. I want to sleep well. I want my body to relax and rejuvenate. I want to reset myself emotionally and physically. I want to wake up feeling energized and eager for my day."

Day No. 18 ~ I am ready to allow all good things into my life

☐ Pre-pave the day

> Dear God, thank you for a brand new opportunity to enjoy life. I want my day to unfold with ease. I want good things to come my way. I want to remember to appreciate people, places and things. I want to be good to myself and others. I want to end this day feeling happy and satisfied. I want to remember at all times that all things are possible.

☐ Meditate (silent or guided, 15-20 mins)

☐ Five things I "Appreciate" today

> *"I love and appreciate..."*

1. _____

2. _____

3. _____

4. _____

5. _____

☐ Three things I want to achieve today

1. _____

2. _____

3. _____

☐ Three things I want the universe to achieve for me

1. _____

2. _____

3. _____

☐ Bless my loved ones

☐ Bless my work

☐ Bless my food

☐ Bless my body

☐ Bless my home

☐ Bless _____

☐ Visualization

"I feel so happy and blessed, my life is really, really good, I am happy where I am and reaching for more."

☐ My thoughts at the end of this day

I enjoyed... I am appreciative of... I am thankful for... I loved... I want more of... I want to be like...

_____

_____

_____

_____

_____

_____

_____

_____

_____

_____

☐   Bed time pre-paving

"I am going to bed now. I want to sleep well. I want
my body to relax and rejuvenate. I want to reset
myself emotionally and physically. I want to wake up
feeling energized and eager for my day."

Day No. 19 ~ The future can be better than the past

☐   Pre-pave the day

> Dear God, thank you for a brand new opportunity to enjoy life. I want my day to unfold with ease. I want good things to come my way. I want to remember to appreciate people, places and things. I want to be good to myself and others. I want to end this day feeling happy and satisfied. I want to remember at all times that all things are possible.

☐   Meditate (silent or guided, 15-20 mins)

☐   Five things I "Appreciate" today

> *"I love and appreciate..."*

1. _____

2. _____

3. _____

4. _____

5. _____

☐   Three things I want to achieve today

1. _____

2. _____

3. _____

☐ Three things I want the universe to achieve for me

1. _____

2. _____

3. _____

☐ Bless my loved ones

☐ Bless my work

☐ Bless my food

☐ Bless my body

☐ Bless my home

☐ Bless _____

☐ Visualization

"I feel so happy and blessed, my life is really, really good, I am happy where I am and reaching for more."

☐ My thoughts at the end of this day

I enjoyed... I am appreciative of... I am thankful for... I loved... I want more of... I want to be like...

_____

_____

_____

_____

_____

_____

_____

_____

_____

_____

_____

☐   Bed time pre-paving

"I am going to bed now. I want to sleep well. I want
my body to relax and rejuvenate. I want to reset
myself emotionally and physically. I want to wake up
feeling energized and eager for my day."

Day No. 20 ~ Joy is my natural state of being

☐   Pre-pave the day

>   Dear God, thank you for a brand new opportunity to enjoy life. I want my day to unfold with ease. I want good things to come my way. I want to remember to appreciate people, places and things. I want to be good to myself and others. I want to end this day feeling happy and satisfied. I want to remember at all times that all things are possible.

☐   Meditate (silent or guided, 15-20 mins)

☐   Five things I "Appreciate" today

>   *"I love and appreciate..."*

1. _____

2. _____

3. _____

4. _____

5. _____

☐   Three things I want to achieve today

1. _____

2. _____

3. _____

☐ Three things I want the universe to achieve for me

1. _____

2. _____

3. _____

☐ Bless my loved ones

☐ Bless my work

☐ Bless my food

☐ Bless my body

☐ Bless my home

☐ Bless _____

☐ Visualization

"I feel so happy and blessed, my life is really, really good, I am happy where I am and reaching for more."

☐ My thoughts at the end of this day

I enjoyed... I am appreciative of... I am thankful for... I loved... I want more of... I want to be like...

_____

_____

_____

_____

_____

_____

_____

_____

_____

_____

☐   Bed time pre-paving

"I am going to bed now. I want to sleep well. I want
my body to relax and rejuvenate. I want to reset
myself emotionally and physically. I want to wake up
feeling energized and eager for my day."

Day No. 21 ~ I want to be one who loves

☐ Pre-pave the day

> Dear God, thank you for a brand new opportunity to enjoy life. I want my day to unfold with ease. I want good things to come my way. I want to remember to appreciate people, places and things. I want to be good to myself and others. I want to end this day feeling happy and satisfied. I want to remember at all times that all things are possible.

☐ Meditate (silent or guided, 15-20 mins)

☐ Five things I "Appreciate" today

> *"I love and appreciate…"*

1. _____

2. _____

3. _____

4. _____

5. _____

☐ Three things I want to achieve today

1. _____

2. _____

3. _____

☐ Three things I want the universe to achieve for me

1. _____

2. _____

3. _____

☐ Bless my loved ones

☐ Bless my work

☐ Bless my food

☐ Bless my body

☐ Bless my home

☐ Bless _____

☐ Visualization

"I feel so happy and blessed, my life is really, really good, I am happy where I am and reaching for more."

☐ My thoughts at the end of this day

I enjoyed... I am appreciative of... I am thankful for... I loved... I want more of... I want to be like...

_____

_____

_____

_____

_____

_____

_____

_____

_____

_____

_____

☐   Bed time pre-paving

"I am going to bed now. I want to sleep well. I want my body to relax and rejuvenate. I want to reset myself emotionally and physically. I want to wake up feeling energized and eager for my day."

Day No. 22 ~ We are all the same, no one is superior to me, no one is inferior to me, we all come from the same Source and we all return to it

☐ Pre-pave the day

> Dear God, thank you for a brand new opportunity to enjoy life. I want my day to unfold with ease. I want good things to come my way. I want to remember to appreciate people, places and things. I want to be good to myself and others. I want to end this day feeling happy and satisfied. I want to remember at all times that all things are possible.

☐ Meditate (silent or guided, 15-20 mins)

☐ Five things I "Appreciate" today

> *"I love and appreciate..."*

1. _____

2. _____

3. _____

4. _____

5. _____

☐ Three things I want to achieve today

1. _____

2. _____

3. _____

☐ Three things I want the universe to achieve for me

    1. _____

    2. _____

    3. _____

☐ Bless my loved ones

☐ Bless my work

☐ Bless my food

☐ Bless my body

☐ Bless my home

☐ Bless _____

☐ Visualization

> "I feel so happy and blessed, my life is really, really good, I am happy where I am and reaching for more."

☐ My thoughts at the end of this day

> I enjoyed... I am appreciative of... I am thankful for... I loved... I want more of... I want to be like...

_____

_____

_____

_____

_____

_____

_____

_____

_____

☐ Bed time pre-paving

"I am going to bed now. I want to sleep well. I want my body to relax and rejuvenate. I want to reset myself emotionally and physically. I want to wake up feeling energized and eager for my day."

Day No. 23 ~ I don't need to prove anything to anyone

☐ Pre-pave the day

> Dear God, thank you for a brand new opportunity to enjoy life. I want my day to unfold with ease. I want good things to come my way. I want to remember to appreciate people, places and things. I want to be good to myself and others. I want to end this day feeling happy and satisfied. I want to remember at all times that all things are possible.

☐ Meditate (silent or guided, 15-20 mins)

☐ Five things I "Appreciate" today

> *"I love and appreciate…"*

1. _____

2. _____

3. _____

4. _____

5. _____

☐ Three things I want to achieve today

1. _____

2. _____

3. _____

☐ Three things I want the universe to achieve for me

1. _____

2. _____

3. _____

☐ Bless my loved ones

☐ Bless my work

☐ Bless my food

☐ Bless my body

☐ Bless my home

☐ Bless _____

☐ Visualization

"I feel so happy and blessed, my life is really, really good, I am happy where I am and reaching for more."

☐ My thoughts at the end of this day

I enjoyed… I am appreciative of… I am thankful for… I loved… I want more of… I want to be like…

_____

_____

_____

_____

_____

_____

_____

_____

_____

_____

_____

☐ Bed time pre-paving

"I am going to bed now. I want to sleep well. I want
my body to relax and rejuvenate. I want to reset
myself emotionally and physically. I want to wake up
feeling energized and eager for my day."

Day No. 24 ~ I am worthy of all good things

☐ Pre-pave the day

> Dear God, thank you for a brand new opportunity to enjoy life. I want my day to unfold with ease. I want good things to come my way. I want to remember to appreciate people, places and things. I want to be good to myself and others. I want to end this day feeling happy and satisfied. I want to remember at all times that all things are possible.

☐ Meditate (silent or guided, 15-20 mins)

☐ Five things I "Appreciate" today

"I love and appreciate..."

1. _____

2. _____

3. _____

4. _____

5. _____

☐ Three things I want to achieve today

1. _____

2. _____

3. _____

☐ Three things I want the universe to achieve for me

1. _____

2. _____

3. _____

☐ Bless my loved ones

☐ Bless my work

☐ Bless my food

☐ Bless my body

☐ Bless my home

☐ Bless _____

☐ Visualization

"I feel so happy and blessed, my life is really, really good, I am happy where I am and reaching for more."

☐ My thoughts at the end of this day

I enjoyed... I am appreciative of... I am thankful for... I loved... I want more of... I want to be like...

_____

_____

_____

_____

_____

_____

_____

_____

_____

_____

☐ Bed time pre-paving

"I am going to bed now. I want to sleep well. I want
my body to relax and rejuvenate. I want to reset
myself emotionally and physically. I want to wake up
feeling energized and eager for my day."

Day No. 25 ~ If I want it, I can have it

☐ Pre-pave the day

Dear God, thank you for a brand new opportunity to enjoy life. I want my day to unfold with ease. I want good things to come my way. I want to remember to appreciate people, places and things. I want to be good to myself and others. I want to end this day feeling happy and satisfied. I want to remember at all times that all things are possible.

☐ Meditate (silent or guided, 15-20 mins)

☐ Five things I "Appreciate" today

"I love and appreciate..."

1. _____

2. _____

3. _____

4. _____

5. _____

☐ Three things I want to achieve today

1. _____

2. _____

3. _____

☐ Three things I want the universe to achieve for me

1. _____

2. _____

3. _____

☐ Bless my loved ones

☐ Bless my work

☐ Bless my food

☐ Bless my body

☐ Bless my home

☐ Bless _____

☐ Visualization

"I feel so happy and blessed, my life is really, really good, I am happy where I am and reaching for more."

☐ My thoughts at the end of this day

I enjoyed... I am appreciative of... I am thankful for... I loved... I want more of... I want to be like...

_____

_____

_____

_____

_____

_____

_____

_____

_____

_____

_____

☐   Bed time pre-paving

"I am going to bed now. I want to sleep well. I want
my body to relax and rejuvenate. I want to reset
myself emotionally and physically. I want to wake up
feeling energized and eager for my day."

Day No. 26 ~ I am blessed with many good things

☐ Pre-pave the day

> Dear God, thank you for a brand new opportunity to enjoy life. I want my day to unfold with ease. I want good things to come my way. I want to remember to appreciate people, places and things. I want to be good to myself and others. I want to end this day feeling happy and satisfied. I want to remember at all times that all things are possible.

☐ Meditate (silent or guided, 15-20 mins)

☐ Five things I "Appreciate" today

"I love and appreciate..."

1. _____

2. _____

3. _____

4. _____

5. _____

☐ Three things I want to achieve today

1. _____

2. _____

3. _____

☐ Three things I want the universe to achieve for me

1. _____

2. _____

3. _____

☐ Bless my loved ones

☐ Bless my work

☐ Bless my food

☐ Bless my body

☐ Bless my home

☐ Bless _____

☐ Visualization

"I feel so happy and blessed, my life is really, really good, I am happy where I am and reaching for more."

☐ My thoughts at the end of this day

I enjoyed... I am appreciative of... I am thankful for... I loved... I want more of... I want to be like...

_____

_____

_____

_____

_____

_____

_____

_____

_____

_____

_____

☐ Bed time pre-paving

"I am going to bed now. I want to sleep well. I want my body to relax and rejuvenate. I want to reset myself emotionally and physically. I want to wake up feeling energized and eager for my day."

Day No. 27 ~ The future can be better than the past

☐ Pre-pave the day

> Dear God, thank you for a brand new opportunity to enjoy life. I want my day to unfold with ease. I want good things to come my way. I want to remember to appreciate people, places and things. I want to be good to myself and others. I want to end this day feeling happy and satisfied. I want to remember at all times that all things are possible.

☐ Meditate (silent or guided, 15-20 mins)

☐ Five things I "Appreciate" today

> *"I love and appreciate..."*

1. _____

2. _____

3. _____

4. _____

5. _____

☐ Three things I want to achieve today

1. _____

2. _____

3. _____

☐ Three things I want the universe to achieve for me

1. _____

2. _____

3. _____

☐ Bless my loved ones

☐ Bless my work

☐ Bless my food

☐ Bless my body

☐ Bless my home

☐ Bless _____

☐ Visualization

"I feel so happy and blessed, my life is really, really good, I am happy where I am and reaching for more."

☐ My thoughts at the end of this day

I enjoyed... I am appreciative of... I am thankful for... I loved... I want more of... I want to be like...

_____

_____

_____

_____

_____

_____

_____

_____

_____

_____

_____

☐   Bed time pre-paving

"I am going to bed now. I want to sleep well. I want
my body to relax and rejuvenate. I want to reset
myself emotionally and physically. I want to wake up
feeling energized and eager for my day."

Day No. 28 ~ I can choose my thoughts

☐　Pre-pave the day

>   Dear God, thank you for a brand new opportunity to
>   enjoy life. I want my day to unfold with ease. I want
>   good things to come my way. I want to remember to
>   appreciate people, places and things. I want to be
>   good to myself and others. I want to end this day
>   feeling happy and satisfied. I want to remember at all
>   times that all things are possible.

☐　Meditate (silent or guided, 15-20 mins)

☐　Five things I "Appreciate" today

>   *"I love and appreciate..."*

1. _____

2. _____

3. _____

4. _____

5. _____

☐　Three things I want to achieve today

1. _____

2. _____

3. _____

☐ Three things I want the universe to achieve for me

1. _____

2. _____

3. _____

☐ Bless my loved ones

☐ Bless my work

☐ Bless my food

☐ Bless my body

☐ Bless my home

☐ Bless _____

☐ Visualization

"I feel so happy and blessed, my life is really, really good, I am happy where I am and reaching for more."

☐ My thoughts at the end of this day

I enjoyed... I am appreciative of... I am thankful for... I loved... I want more of... I want to be like...

_____

_____

_____

_____

_____

_____

_____

_____

_____

_____

_____

☐   Bed time pre-paving

"I am going to bed now. I want to sleep well. I want
my body to relax and rejuvenate. I want to reset
myself emotionally and physically. I want to wake up
feeling energized and eager for my day."

Day No. 29 ~ I want to be one who creates a happy day every day

☐ Pre-pave the day

> Dear God, thank you for a brand new opportunity to enjoy life. I want my day to unfold with ease. I want good things to come my way. I want to remember to appreciate people, places and things. I want to be good to myself and others. I want to end this day feeling happy and satisfied. I want to remember at all times that all things are possible.

☐ Meditate (silent or guided, 15-20 mins)

☐ Five things I "Appreciate" today

"I love and appreciate..."

1. _____

2. _____

3. _____

4. _____

5. _____

☐ Three things I want to achieve today

1. _____

2. _____

3. _____

☐ Three things I want the universe to achieve for me

   1. _____

   2. _____

   3. _____

☐ Bless my loved ones

☐ Bless my work

☐ Bless my food

☐ Bless my body

☐ Bless my home

☐ Bless _____

☐ Visualization

   "I feel so happy and blessed, my life is really, really good, I am happy where I am and reaching for more."

☐ My thoughts at the end of this day

   I enjoyed... I am appreciative of... I am thankful for... I loved... I want more of... I want to be like...

   _____

   _____

_____

_____

_____

_____

_____

_____

_____

_____

_____

☐ Bed time pre-paving

"I am going to bed now. I want to sleep well. I want
my body to relax and rejuvenate. I want to reset
myself emotionally and physically. I want to wake up
feeling energized and eager for my day."

Day No. 30 ~ I want to feel freedom and joy

☐ Pre-pave the day

> Dear God, thank you for a brand new opportunity to enjoy life. I want my day to unfold with ease. I want good things to come my way. I want to remember to appreciate people, places and things. I want to be good to myself and others. I want to end this day feeling happy and satisfied. I want to remember at all times that all things are possible.

☐ Meditate (silent or guided, 15-20 mins)

☐ Five things I "Appreciate" today

> *"I love and appreciate…"*

1. _____

2. _____

3. _____

4. _____

5. _____

☐ Three things I want to achieve today

1. _____

2. _____

3. _____

☐ Three things I want the universe to achieve for me

1. _____

2. _____

3. _____

☐ Bless my loved ones

☐ Bless my work

☐ Bless my food

☐ Bless my body

☐ Bless my home

☐ Bless _____

☐ Visualization

"I feel so happy and blessed, my life is really, really good, I am happy where I am and reaching for more."

☐ My thoughts at the end of this day

I enjoyed... I am appreciative of... I am thankful for... I loved... I want more of... I want to be like...

_____

_____

_____

_____

_____

_____

_____

_____

_____

_____

_____

☐ Bed time pre-paving

"I am going to bed now. I want to sleep well. I want my body to relax and rejuvenate. I want to reset myself emotionally and physically. I want to wake up feeling energized and eager for my day."

Day No. 31 ~ I want to feel love and appreciation

☐ Pre-pave the day

> Dear God, thank you for a brand new opportunity to enjoy life. I want my day to unfold with ease. I want good things to come my way. I want to remember to appreciate people, places and things. I want to be good to myself and others. I want to end this day feeling happy and satisfied. I want to remember at all times that all things are possible.

☐ Meditate (silent or guided, 15-20 mins)

☐ Five things I "Appreciate" today

"I love and appreciate..."

1. _____

2. _____

3. _____

4. _____

5. _____

☐ Three things I want to achieve today

1. _____

2. _____

3. _____

☐ Three things I want the universe to achieve for me

1. _____

2. _____

3. _____

☐ Bless my loved ones

☐ Bless my work

☐ Bless my food

☐ Bless my body

☐ Bless my home

☐ Bless _____

☐ Visualization

"I feel so happy and blessed, my life is really, really good, I am happy where I am and reaching for more."

☐ My thoughts at the end of this day

I enjoyed... I am appreciative of... I am thankful for... I loved... I want more of... I want to be like...

_____

_____

_____

_____

_____

_____

_____

_____

_____

_____

_____

☐   Bed time pre-paving

> "I am going to bed now. I want to sleep well. I want
> my body to relax and rejuvenate. I want to reset
> myself emotionally and physically. I want to wake up
> feeling energized and eager for my day."

Day No. 32 ~ I am ready to give up all those beliefs that no longer serve me

☐ Pre-pave the day

> Dear God, thank you for a brand new opportunity to enjoy life. I want my day to unfold with ease. I want good things to come my way. I want to remember to appreciate people, places and things. I want to be good to myself and others. I want to end this day feeling happy and satisfied. I want to remember at all times that all things are possible.

☐ Meditate (silent or guided, 15-20 mins)

☐ Five things I "Appreciate" today

> *"I love and appreciate..."*

1. _____

2. _____

3. _____

4. _____

5. _____

☐ Three things I want to achieve today

1. _____

2. _____

3. _____

☐ Three things I want the universe to achieve for me

1. _____

2. _____

3. _____

☐ Bless my loved ones

☐ Bless my work

☐ Bless my food

☐ Bless my body

☐ Bless my home

☐ Bless _____

☐ Visualization

"I feel so happy and blessed, my life is really, really good, I am happy where I am and reaching for more."

☐ My thoughts at the end of this day

I enjoyed... I am appreciative of... I am thankful for... I loved... I want more of... I want to be like...

_____

_____

_____

_____

_____

_____

_____

_____

_____

_____

_____

☐   Bed time pre-paving

> "I am going to bed now. I want to sleep well. I want
> my body to relax and rejuvenate. I want to reset
> myself emotionally and physically. I want to wake up
> feeling energized and eager for my day."

Day No. 33 ~ I want to be of value to others and to feel my own value

☐   Pre-pave the day

> Dear God, thank you for a brand new opportunity to enjoy life. I want my day to unfold with ease. I want good things to come my way. I want to remember to appreciate people, places and things. I want to be good to myself and others. I want to end this day feeling happy and satisfied. I want to remember at all times that all things are possible.

☐   Meditate (silent or guided, 15-20 mins)

☐   Five things I "Appreciate" today

> *"I love and appreciate..."*

1. _____

2. _____

3. _____

4. _____

5. _____

☐   Three things I want to achieve today

1. _____

2. _____

3. _____

☐ Three things I want the universe to achieve for me

1. _____

2. _____

3. _____

☐ Bless my loved ones

☐ Bless my work

☐ Bless my food

☐ Bless my body

☐ Bless my home

☐ Bless _____

☐ Visualization

"I feel so happy and blessed, my life is really, really good, I am happy where I am and reaching for more."

☐ My thoughts at the end of this day

I enjoyed... I am appreciative of... I am thankful for... I loved... I want more of... I want to be like...

_____

_____

_____

_____

_____

_____

_____

_____

_____

_____

☐   Bed time pre-paving

"I am going to bed now. I want to sleep well. I want
my body to relax and rejuvenate. I want to reset
myself emotionally and physically. I want to wake up
feeling energized and eager for my day."

Day No. 34 ~ My success is certain

☐ Pre-pave the day

> Dear God, thank you for a brand new opportunity to enjoy life. I want my day to unfold with ease. I want good things to come my way. I want to remember to appreciate people, places and things. I want to be good to myself and others. I want to end this day feeling happy and satisfied. I want to remember at all times that all things are possible.

☐ Meditate (silent or guided, 15-20 mins)

☐ Five things I "Appreciate" today

"I love and appreciate…"

1. _____

2. _____

3. _____

4. _____

5. _____

☐ Three things I want to achieve today

1. _____

2. _____

3. _____

☐ Three things I want the universe to achieve for me

1. _____

2. _____

3. _____

☐ Bless my loved ones

☐ Bless my work

☐ Bless my food

☐ Bless my body

☐ Bless my home

☐ Bless _____

☐ Visualization

"I feel so happy and blessed, my life is really, really good, I am happy where I am and reaching for more."

☐ My thoughts at the end of this day

I enjoyed... I am appreciative of... I am thankful for... I loved... I want more of... I want to be like...

_____

_____

_____

_____

_____

_____

_____

_____

_____

_____

_____

☐   Bed time pre-paving

"I am going to bed now. I want to sleep well. I want
my body to relax and rejuvenate. I want to reset
myself emotionally and physically. I want to wake up
feeling energized and eager for my day."

Day No. 35 ~ This is my time to receive all the things I have been asking for

☐   Pre-pave the day

> Dear God, thank you for a brand new opportunity to enjoy life. I want my day to unfold with ease. I want good things to come my way. I want to remember to appreciate people, places and things. I want to be good to myself and others. I want to end this day feeling happy and satisfied. I want to remember at all times that all things are possible.

☐   Meditate (silent or guided, 15-20 mins)

☐   Five things I "Appreciate" today

> *"I love and appreciate..."*

1. _____

2. _____

3. _____

4. _____

5. _____

☐   Three things I want to achieve today

1. _____

2. _____

3. _____

☐ Three things I want the universe to achieve for me

1. _____

2. _____

3. _____

☐ Bless my loved ones

☐ Bless my work

☐ Bless my food

☐ Bless my body

☐ Bless my home

☐ Bless _____

☐ Visualization

"I feel so happy and blessed, my life is really, really good, I am happy where I am and reaching for more."

☐ My thoughts at the end of this day

I enjoyed... I am appreciative of... I am thankful for... I loved... I want more of... I want to be like...

_____

_____

_____

_____

_____

_____

_____

_____

_____

_____

_____

☐ Bed time pre-paving

"I am going to bed now. I want to sleep well. I want my body to relax and rejuvenate. I want to reset myself emotionally and physically. I want to wake up feeling energized and eager for my day."

Day No. 36 ~ I am willing to smile more and laugh more

☐ Pre-pave the day

> Dear God, thank you for a brand new opportunity to enjoy life. I want my day to unfold with ease. I want good things to come my way. I want to remember to appreciate people, places and things. I want to be good to myself and others. I want to end this day feeling happy and satisfied. I want to remember at all times that all things are possible.

☐ Meditate (silent or guided, 15-20 mins)

☐ Five things I "Appreciate" today

> *"I love and appreciate..."*

1. _____

2. _____

3. _____

4. _____

5. _____

☐ Three things I want to achieve today

1. _____

2. _____

3. _____

☐ Three things I want the universe to achieve for me

1. _____

2. _____

3. _____

☐ Bless my loved ones

☐ Bless my work

☐ Bless my food

☐ Bless my body

☐ Bless my home

☐ Bless _____

☐ Visualization

"I feel so happy and blessed, my life is really, really good, I am happy where I am and reaching for more."

☐ My thoughts at the end of this day

I enjoyed... I am appreciative of... I am thankful for... I loved... I want more of... I want to be like...

_____

_____

_____

_____

_____

_____

_____

_____

_____

_____

_____

☐   Bed time pre-paving

> "I am going to bed now. I want to sleep well. I want
> my body to relax and rejuvenate. I want to reset
> myself emotionally and physically. I want to wake up
> feeling energized and eager for my day."

Day No. 37 ~ Today I want my positive vibration to bring me new possibilities

☐ Pre-pave the day

> Dear God, thank you for a brand new opportunity to enjoy life. I want my day to unfold with ease. I want good things to come my way. I want to remember to appreciate people, places and things. I want to be good to myself and others. I want to end this day feeling happy and satisfied. I want to remember at all times that all things are possible.

☐ Meditate (silent or guided, 15-20 mins)

☐ Five things I "Appreciate" today

"I love and appreciate..."

1. _____

2. _____

3. _____

4. _____

5. _____

☐ Three things I want to achieve today

1. _____

2. _____

3. _____

☐ Three things I want the universe to achieve for me

1. _____

2. _____

3. _____

☐ Bless my loved ones

☐ Bless my work

☐ Bless my food

☐ Bless my body

☐ Bless my home

☐ Bless _____

☐ Visualization

"I feel so happy and blessed, my life is really, really good, I am happy where I am and reaching for more."

☐ My thoughts at the end of this day

I enjoyed... I am appreciative of... I am thankful for... I loved... I want more of... I want to be like...

_____

_____

_____

_____

_____

_____

_____

_____

_____

_____

☐   Bed time pre-paving

"I am going to bed now. I want to sleep well. I want
my body to relax and rejuvenate. I want to reset
myself emotionally and physically. I want to wake up
feeling energized and eager for my day."

Day No. 38 ~ I don't need things to change to feel good

☐ Pre-pave the day

> Dear God, thank you for a brand new opportunity to enjoy life. I want my day to unfold with ease. I want good things to come my way. I want to remember to appreciate people, places and things. I want to be good to myself and others. I want to end this day feeling happy and satisfied. I want to remember at all times that all things are possible.

☐ Meditate (silent or guided, 15-20 mins)

☐ Five things I "Appreciate" today

"I love and appreciate..."

1. _____

2. _____

3. _____

4. _____

5. _____

☐ Three things I want to achieve today

1. _____

2. _____

3. _____

☐ Three things I want the universe to achieve for me

1. _____

2. _____

3. _____

☐ Bless my loved ones

☐ Bless my work

☐ Bless my food

☐ Bless my body

☐ Bless my home

☐ Bless _____

☐ Visualization

"I feel so happy and blessed, my life is really, really good, I am happy where I am and reaching for more."

☐ My thoughts at the end of this day

I enjoyed... I am appreciative of... I am thankful for... I loved... I want more of... I want to be like...

_____

_____

_____

_____

_____

_____

_____

_____

_____

_____

_____

☐   Bed time pre-paving

"I am going to bed now. I want to sleep well. I want
my body to relax and rejuvenate. I want to reset
myself emotionally and physically. I want to wake up
feeling energized and eager for my day."

Day No. 39 ~ My work is to appreciate and I know I can do that

☐ Pre-pave the day

> Dear God, thank you for a brand new opportunity to enjoy life. I want my day to unfold with ease. I want good things to come my way. I want to remember to appreciate people, places and things. I want to be good to myself and others. I want to end this day feeling happy and satisfied. I want to remember at all times that all things are possible.

☐ Meditate (silent or guided, 15-20 mins)

☐ Five things I "Appreciate" today

"I love and appreciate..."

1. _____

2. _____

3. _____

4. _____

5. _____

☐ Three things I want to achieve today

1. _____

2. _____

3. ☐ _____

☐ Three things I want the universe to achieve for me

    1. _____

    2. _____

    3. _____

☐ Bless my loved ones

☐ Bless my work

☐ Bless my food

☐ Bless my body

☐ Bless my home

☐ Bless _____

☐ Visualization

    "I feel so happy and blessed, my life is really, really good, I am happy where I am and reaching for more."

☐ My thoughts at the end of this day

    I enjoyed... I am appreciative of... I am thankful for... I loved... I want more of... I want to be like...

    _____

    _____

_____

_____

_____

_____

_____

_____

_____

_____

_____

☐   Bed time pre-paving

> "I am going to bed now. I want to sleep well. I want
> my body to relax and rejuvenate. I want to reset
> myself emotionally and physically. I want to wake up
> feeling energized and eager for my day."

Day No. 40 ~ I think I'm ready to bring enthusiasm into my life

☐ Pre-pave the day

> Dear God, thank you for a brand new opportunity to enjoy life. I want my day to unfold with ease. I want good things to come my way. I want to remember to appreciate people, places and things. I want to be good to myself and others. I want to end this day feeling happy and satisfied. I want to remember at all times that all things are possible.

☐ Meditate (silent or guided, 15-20 mins)

☐ Five things I "Appreciate" today

"I love and appreciate..."

1. _____

2. _____

3. _____

4. _____

5. _____

☐ Three things I want to achieve today

1. _____

2. _____

3. _____

☐ Three things I want the universe to achieve for me

    1. _____

    2. _____

    3. _____

☐ Bless my loved ones

☐ Bless my work

☐ Bless my food

☐ Bless my body

☐ Bless my home

☐ Bless _____

☐ Visualization

> "I feel so happy and blessed, my life is really, really good, I am happy where I am and reaching for more."

☐ My thoughts at the end of this day

> I enjoyed... I am appreciative of... I am thankful for... I loved... I want more of... I want to be like...

_____

_____

_____

_____

_____

_____

_____

_____

_____

_____

☐ Bed time pre-paving

"I am going to bed now. I want to sleep well. I want my body to relax and rejuvenate. I want to reset myself emotionally and physically. I want to wake up feeling energized and eager for my day."

The 40 day conclusion

Here we are at the end of our 40 day workout.

How do you feel?

How you feel is the best measure of your success. If you are feeling better than you did when we started this journey together 40 days ago then you have put the process of improvement into place.

Even if you can't really feel a discernible shift in the way you feel, know that you have done your part and things are moving forward in the direction you want. Sometimes it can be a while before the results become obvious enough that you can see them. Just like the seed that starts growing below the surface of the soil and becomes obvious to you only when it breaks ground.

If you like you can do a check to see if you can feel the shift that has surely taken place.

On a scale of one to ten, ten being best identify where you are on the following aspects of your life:

Health   ____

Money   ____

Relationships   ____

Self-worth   ____

Personality   ____

Career   ____

Joy   ____

Freedom   ____

Other subject important to me _____, _____

You have created a major vibrational shift in your energy by being consistent over the 40 days and pretty soon you will begin to see the evidence of the work you have done.

Don't stop here – keep going. Take some of the exercises you have done over the 40 days and make them your way of life. Do them anyway.

It is my promise to you that your life will never be the same again.

Much love and appreciation,
Zehra

PS: If you have found value in this book – leave a review on Amazon to help others decide if this book is for them.

Remember to join the Unlimited – Law of Attraction Coaching and Support Group on Facebook.

FREE to join if you have purchased a Kindle or Print copy of this book.

About the author

Zehra Mahoon lives in Ontario, Canada with her two beautiful children, Kinza and Faris, a hyper cat called Izzy, a lazy cat called Sitka and Stella the forever puppy.

Zehra loves her small town Oshawa and over the past fourteen years she has finally adjusted to the snow and cold weather in Ontario, but always welcomes a timely opportunity to get away to warmer places preferably with lots of old trees, rocks and water, good food and vibrant colours.

Zehra teaches weekly meditation classes at the local library and offers an open discussion session. She loves to teach, coach and write for her blog, as well as other journals and magazines. Zehra is an accomplished speaker and often makes television appearances. Aside from teaching the law of attraction, and offering financial advice , Zehra loves to cook and entertain and have fun with each new day of her life.

To find out more about Zehra and her work please visit her website.

Zehra's other books include:

How to Pray so That God Listens

100 PRAYERS FOR ULTIMATE JOY & SUCCESS IN LIFE

ZEHRA MAHOON

A book that explains prayer. It explains how God's system for granting wishes works. It explains why some people get things easily while other people don't. It explains how to pray so that all your prayers will be answered.

Thrive – Free yourself from Worry, Anger and other negative emotions

Free Yourself from Worry, Anger and Other Negative Emotions

By Zehra Mahoon

Many books have been written about anger management and over coming worry and anxiety and about what to think and believe and how to act, but three things set this book apart from the rest:

1. The depiction of the thinking process in the form of illustrations that make it easy to understand how our thoughts impact our results; 2. A method that helps us to identify the beliefs that operate under the surface and control our lives without our knowing it; and 3. A simple four step process that helps to deactivate negative beliefs permanently so that we can thrive.

The end result: freedom from worry, anxiety, and anger and a set of thinking exercises that can be used in every situation you would ever encounter in life.

Is this Apple from my Tree? is a book about parenting.

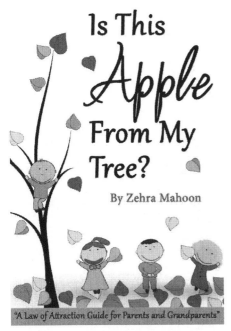

By Zehra Mahoon

"A Law of Attraction Guide for Parents and Grandparents"

Being a good parent is as much about looking after yourself as it is about looking after your child.

This book will help you to:

1. Become a confident, relaxed and happy parent who enjoys every moment of having children.

2. Raise children with positive belief systems that enable them to be confident, happy, healthy, creative, and successful.

Zehra shares many practical examples of situation that she encountered with her own children how she dealt with them successfully to help you understand how your power of positive thinking impacts your children without ever having to tell them to change or do anything differently.

Peace Within is a book about meditation

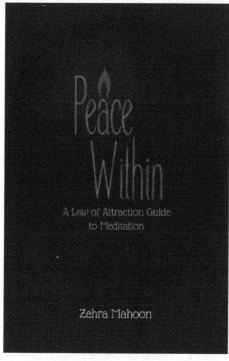

Meditation is made out to be way more difficult than it truly is. One of the reasons for this is that there are so many different ways being taught. The purpose of this little book is to dig down to the foundation of the process of meditation and talk about why things are done in various different ways. The fewer the rules and rituals the easier it is.

This book makes meditation easy.

If you have wanted to learn meditation and felt that you could not turn off your thoughts then this book is meant for you for you are about to learn that there is really no need for you to ever turn your thoughts off – in fact you can't – that's the equivalent of telling your heart to stop pumping blood!

The Prosperity Puzzle: Your relationship with money and how to improve it

Prosperity Puzzle

"Your Relationship with Money and How to Improve It."

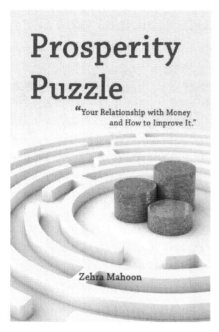

Zehra Mahoon

Have you ever wondered why some people who have the skills and the education and everything else they need to be successful aren't and others who have far less qualifications are?

Have you ever wondered why one business in the same industry with the same product succeeds and another doesn't?

That's what this book is all about – it explains how the way we think about money has an impact upon how much money flows into our lives.

It explains how to work on and remove the negative beliefs that are standing between you and prosperity. You deserve to be rich, and anything that you want is possible.

Win: a law of attraction guide to winning

A LAW OF ATTRACTION
GUIDE TO WINNING
THE LOTTERY

ZEHRA
MAHOON

The Law of Attraction is always working, whether you use it consciously or not.

This powerful law is at the base of why things out the way they do.

This book will help you to improve your understanding of the nine important elements that contribute towards winning anything – especially the lottery, accompanied with step wise guide to making them work for you.

This book will give you an understanding of what you need to stop doing in order to start winning the lottery and so much more.

If thoughts create then... why do bad things happen to good people?
This is a FREE BOOK

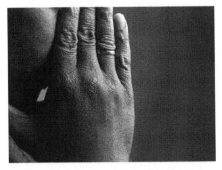

IF THOUGHTS
CREATE THEN...

WHY DO BAD THINGS
HAPPEN TO GOOD PEOPLE?

ZEHRA
MAHOON

The purpose of this book is to explain why bad things happen to good people, and how to learn to control your thought process in order to create a future that you really want to live.

You can download a free pdf copy of this book at www.zmahoon.com

Zehra's books are available in digital and print formats through Amazon.com

One Last Thing...

If you enjoyed this book or found it useful I would truly appreciate it if you would post a short review on Amazon. Your support really does make a difference and I read all the reviews personally so I can get your feedback and make this book even better.
Much love and appreciation,
Zehra

Made in the USA
San Bernardino, CA
23 May 2017